Thanks:

Jeffery Chance

William Chance

Sandra Stockton

and

Mildred Jean Jeffers

Thanks for the knowledge:

California State University Los Angeles

Los Angeles County Museum of Art

Pasadena City College

Armory Center for the Arts

Table of Contents

We must acknowledge what he need to

erase

For history is more than a time, face, and

place

Make connections. Understand the context

Maybe, we can then reset.

Idi Amin

Such a strange man; the big media fool

Some may be false, but most of it's true.

One half a million now dead so it's said

No Obote to be Uganda's head.

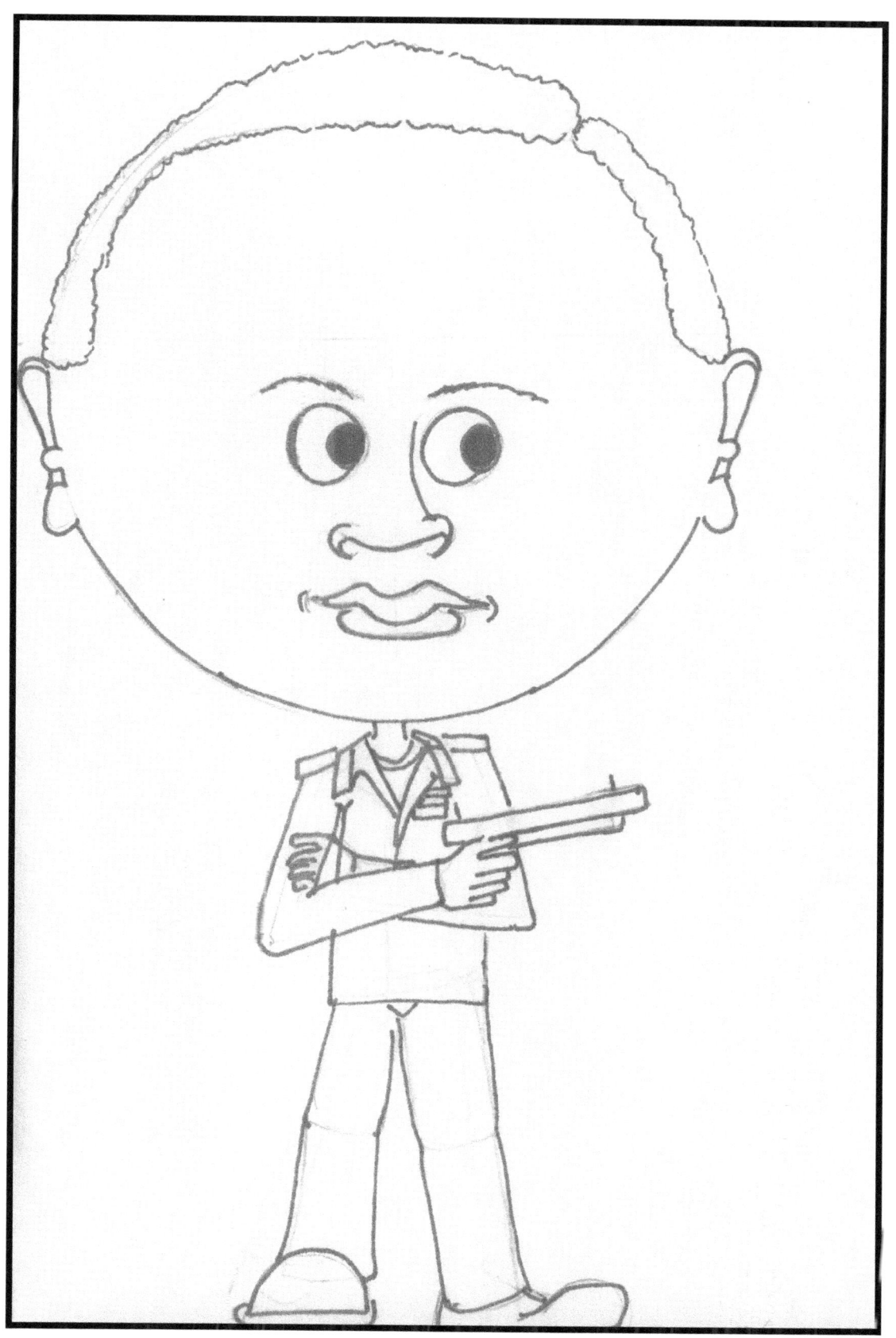

Elizabeth Bathory

Maidens walk wordlessly within my lair

Drain the essence with no common

sense

My desire for beauty is my defense

royally. I gaily descent the stair.

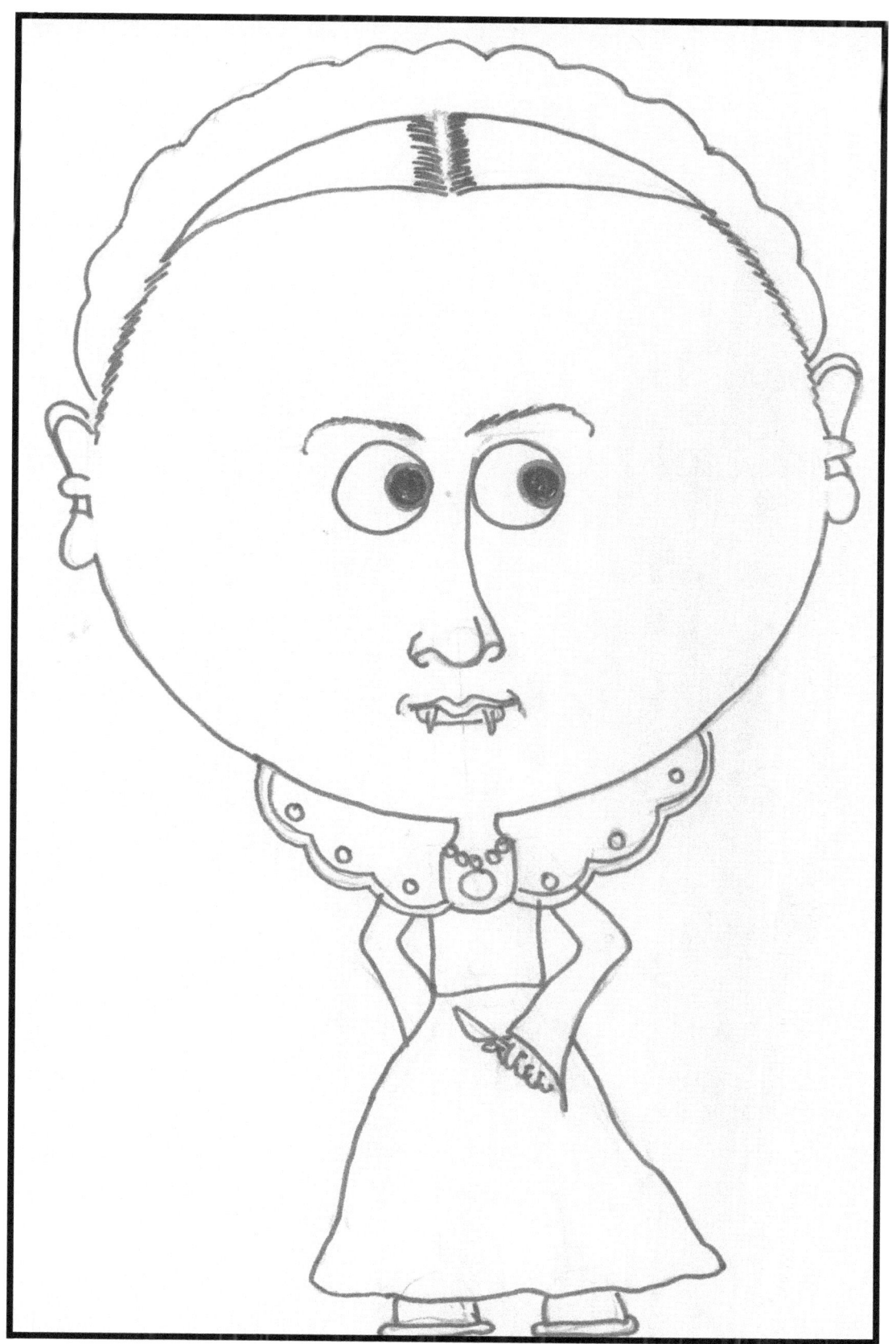

Caligula

Mistress sisters pawned to paying misters

Accused innocents treated like blisters

If what they say was the truth little Boot

You were strangled by a sadistic root.

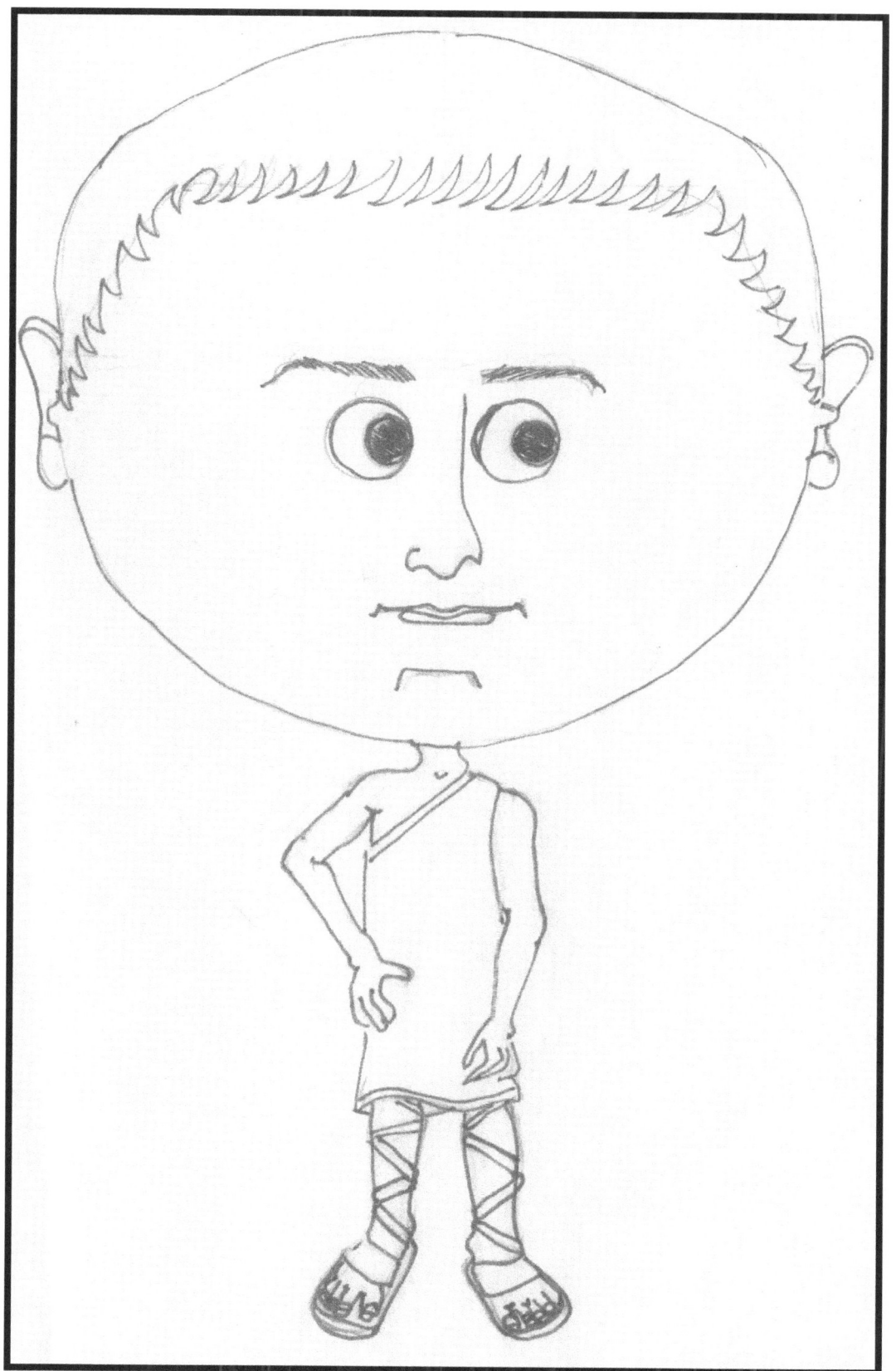

Fidel Castro

The revolutionary burst on the scene

Puffing on a cigar and wearing khaki green

They said he was a killer and a tyrant

So we banned the Cuban tobacco plant.

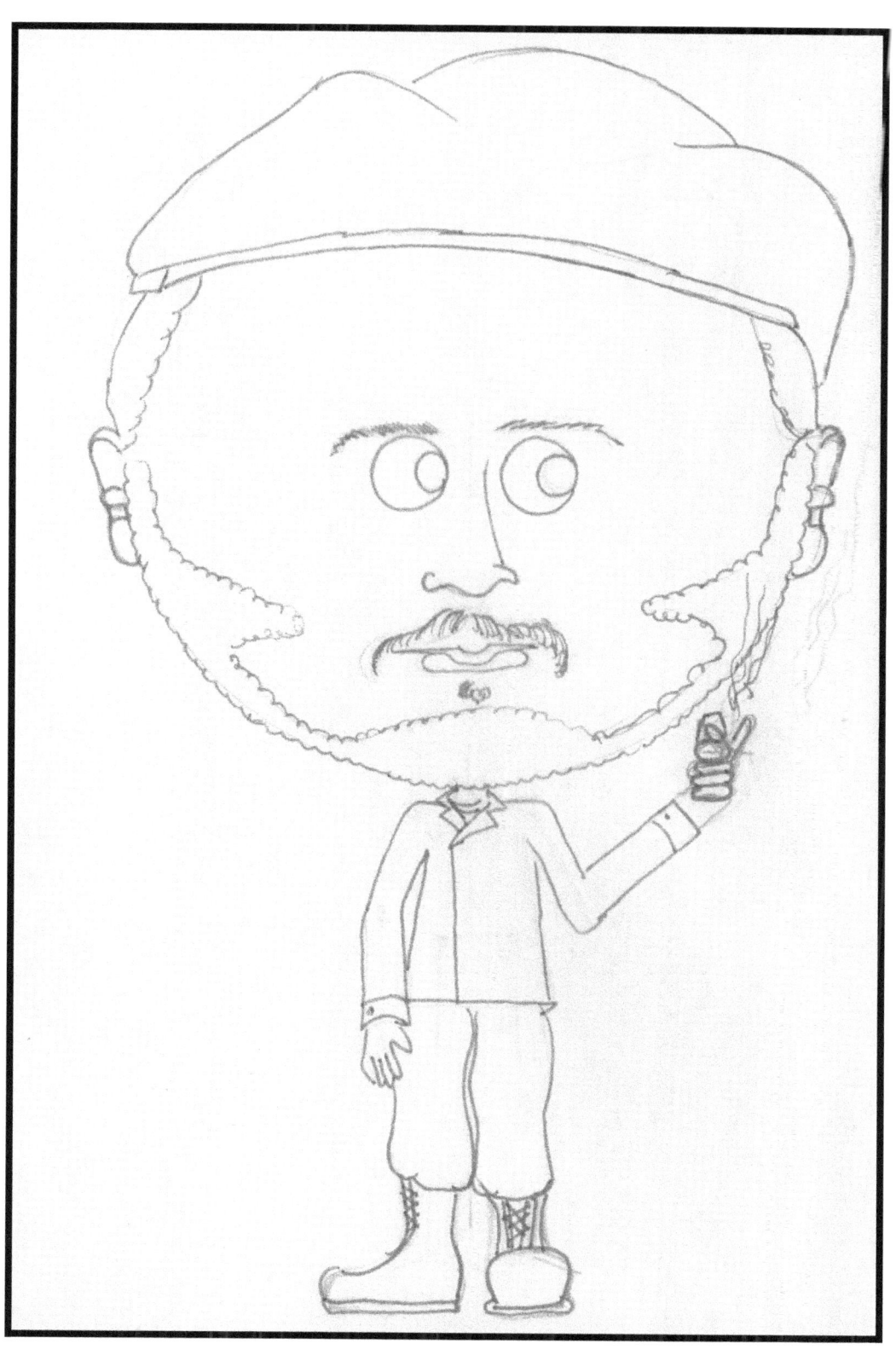

Laurent Gbagbo

You taught lessons you did not learn

Cocoa covers white sands are now filled
with blood

Civil wars and sanctioned genocide
burned

Overwhelming dissent comes like a
flood

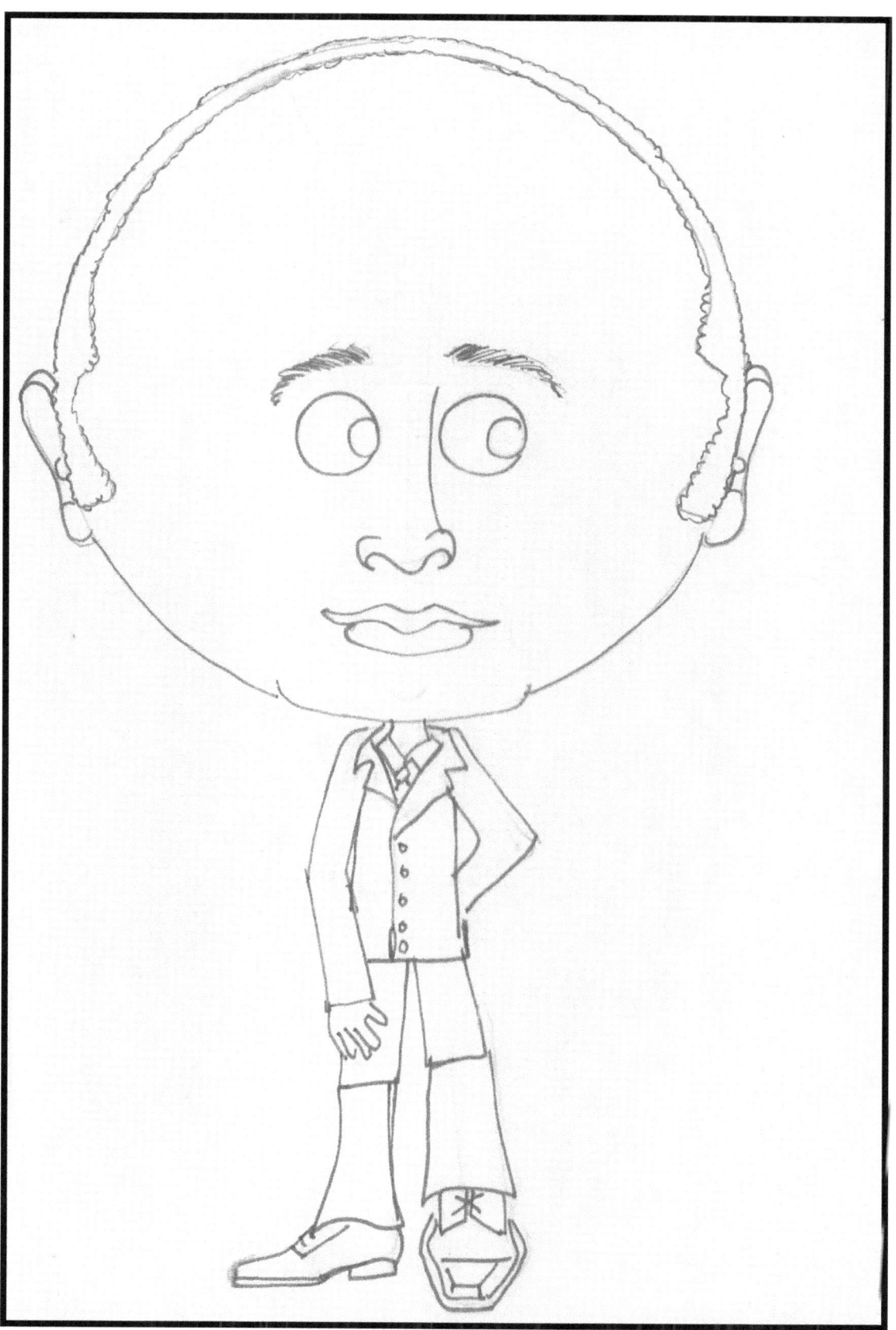

Andrew Jackson

This land is our land, but it's in your
hands

We tearfully leave our home, and you're
revered

Ignorance is a fierce force to be feared.

Native Americans form bands that say,
"Two tens please."

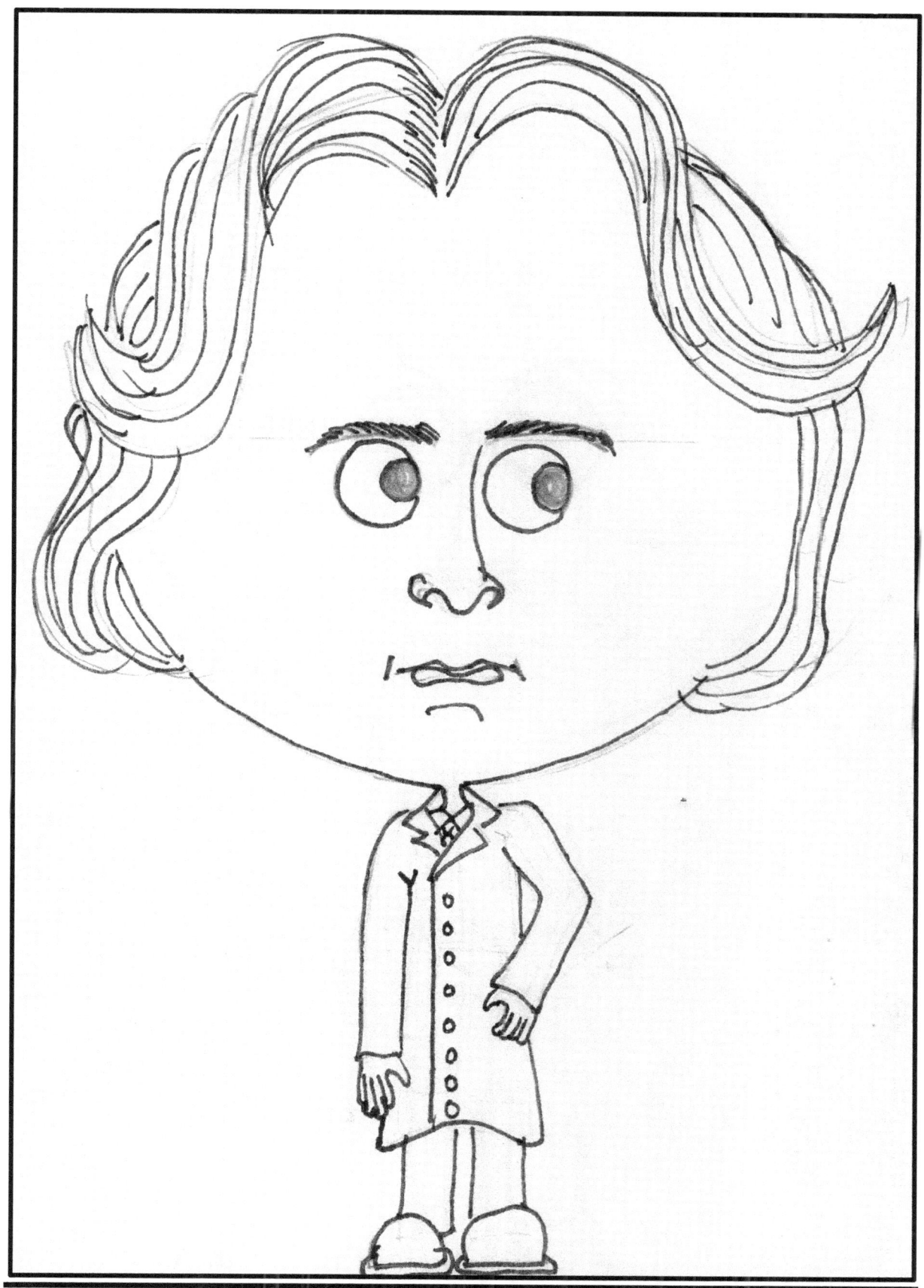

Genghis Khan

This Mongolian was not chicken

Ancient Asians saw the death toll
thicken

However, what he did the best

Was give no maiden a decent rest

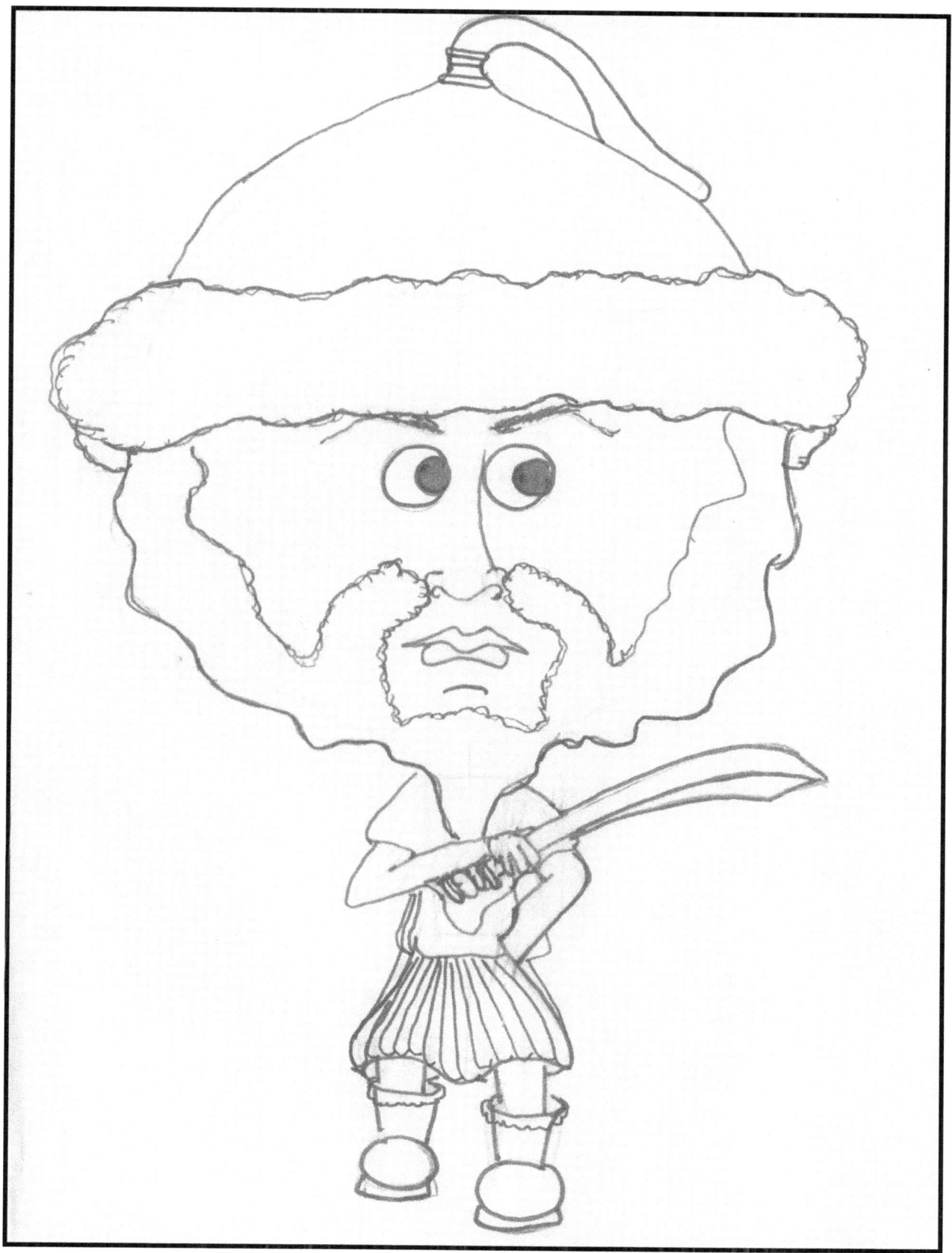

Senator Joseph McCarthey

Joseph told us better dead than reddish

He seemed to have a communist fetish

Career killer and terror filler

1950s inquisition griller

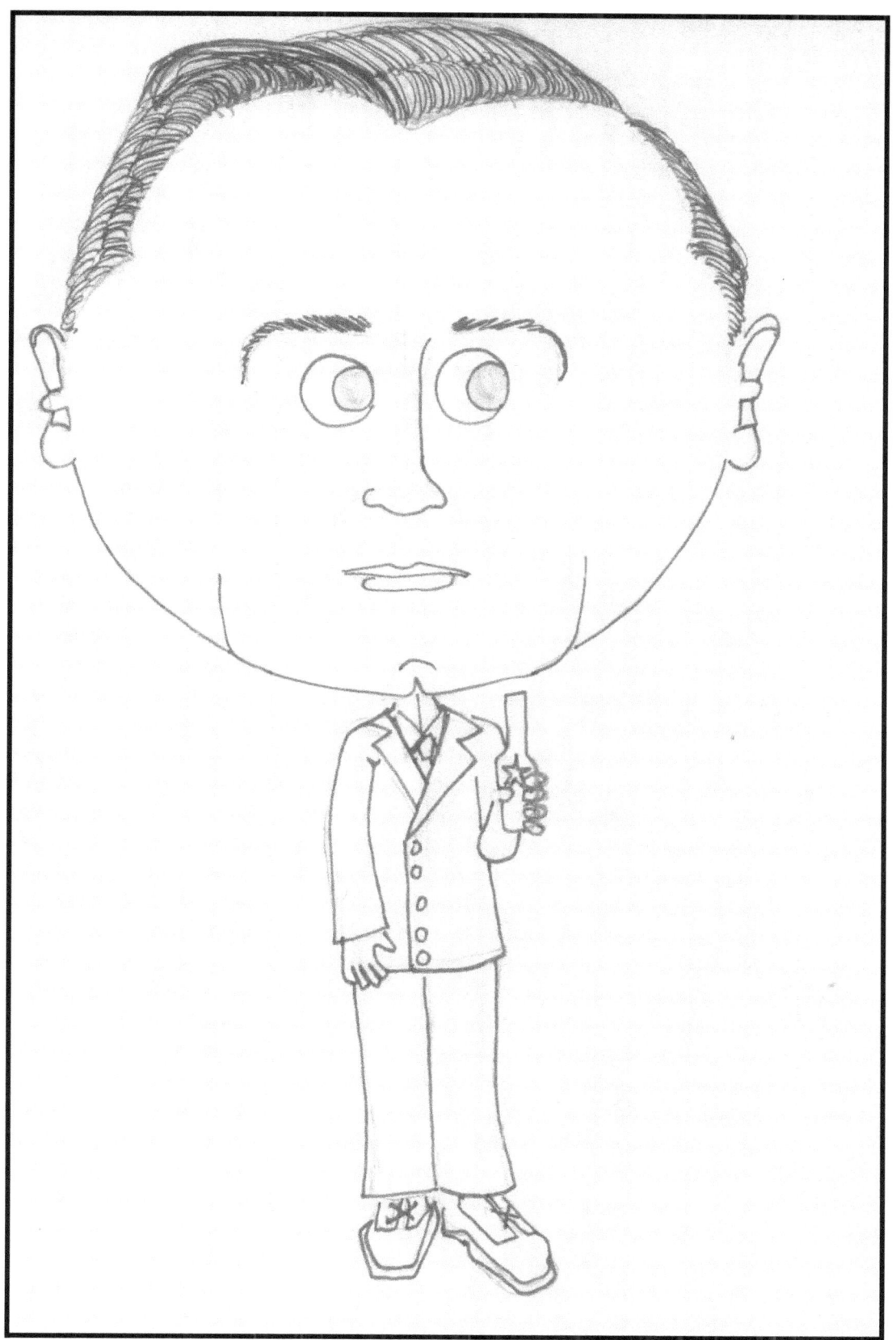

Francisco Pizzaro

I am the sun king; yes this is true

I will slaughter and subjugate you

Long live Spain and its kings reign

I if I could, I would do it again

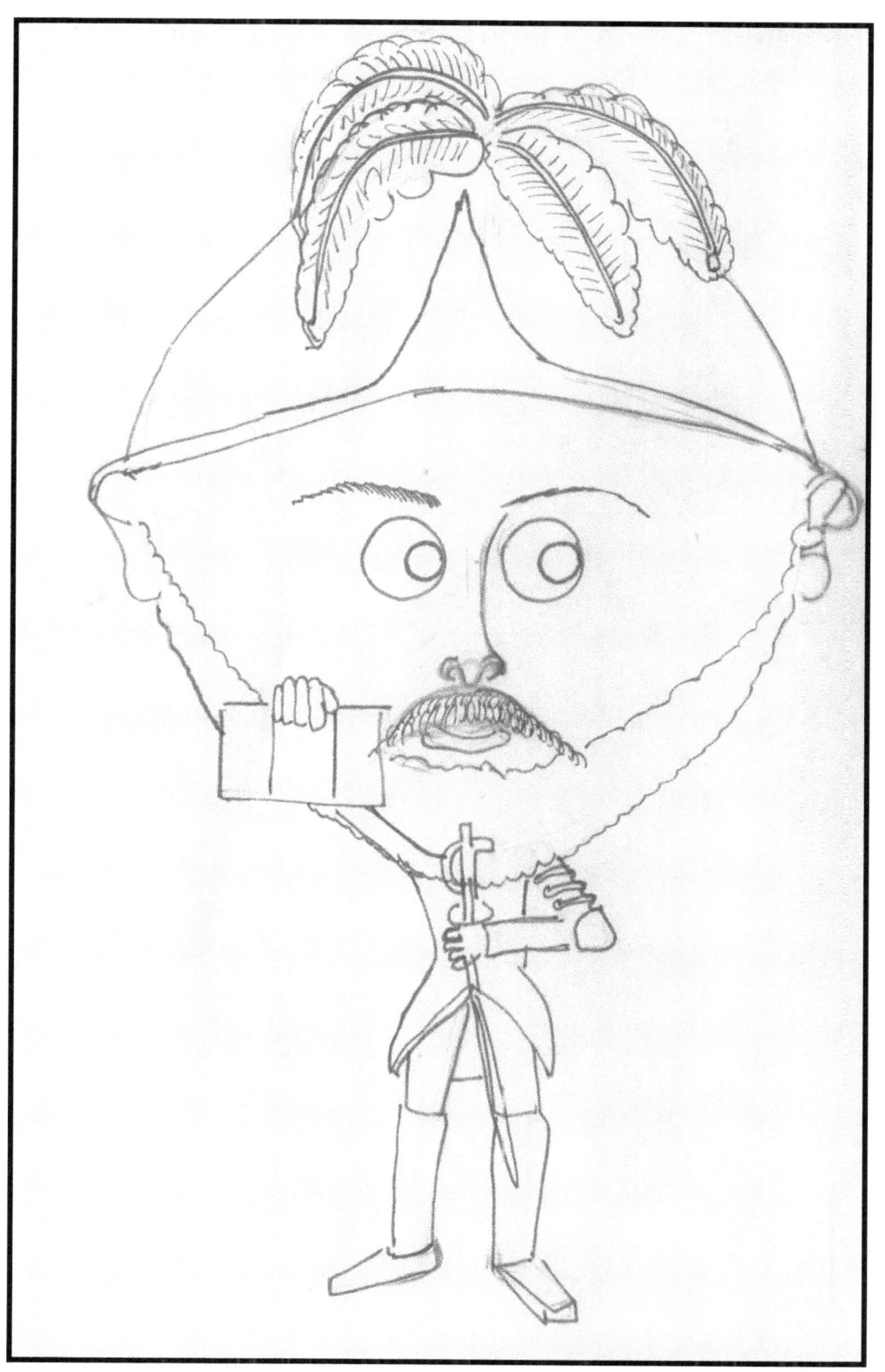

Joseph Stalin

A little twisted in body and mind

Somewhat criminal from the very start

Inevitably grew cruel and unkind

Red Terror alone showed he had no

heart

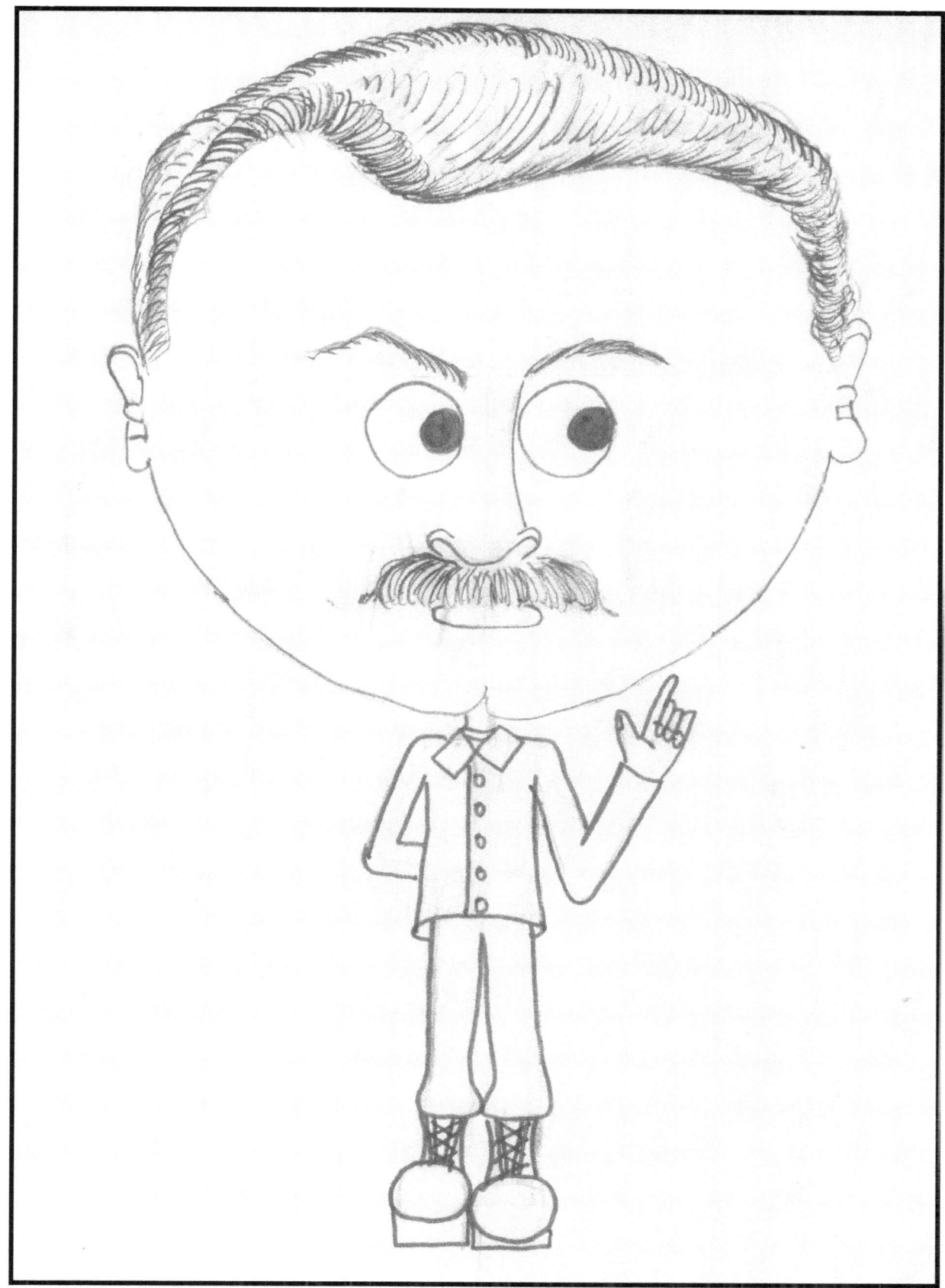

Adolf Hitler and Benito Mussolini

I kiss you dearly in Italy

I admire that stance in your tight black
    pants

You had my protection near Tripoli

Still you danced the hangman's dance.

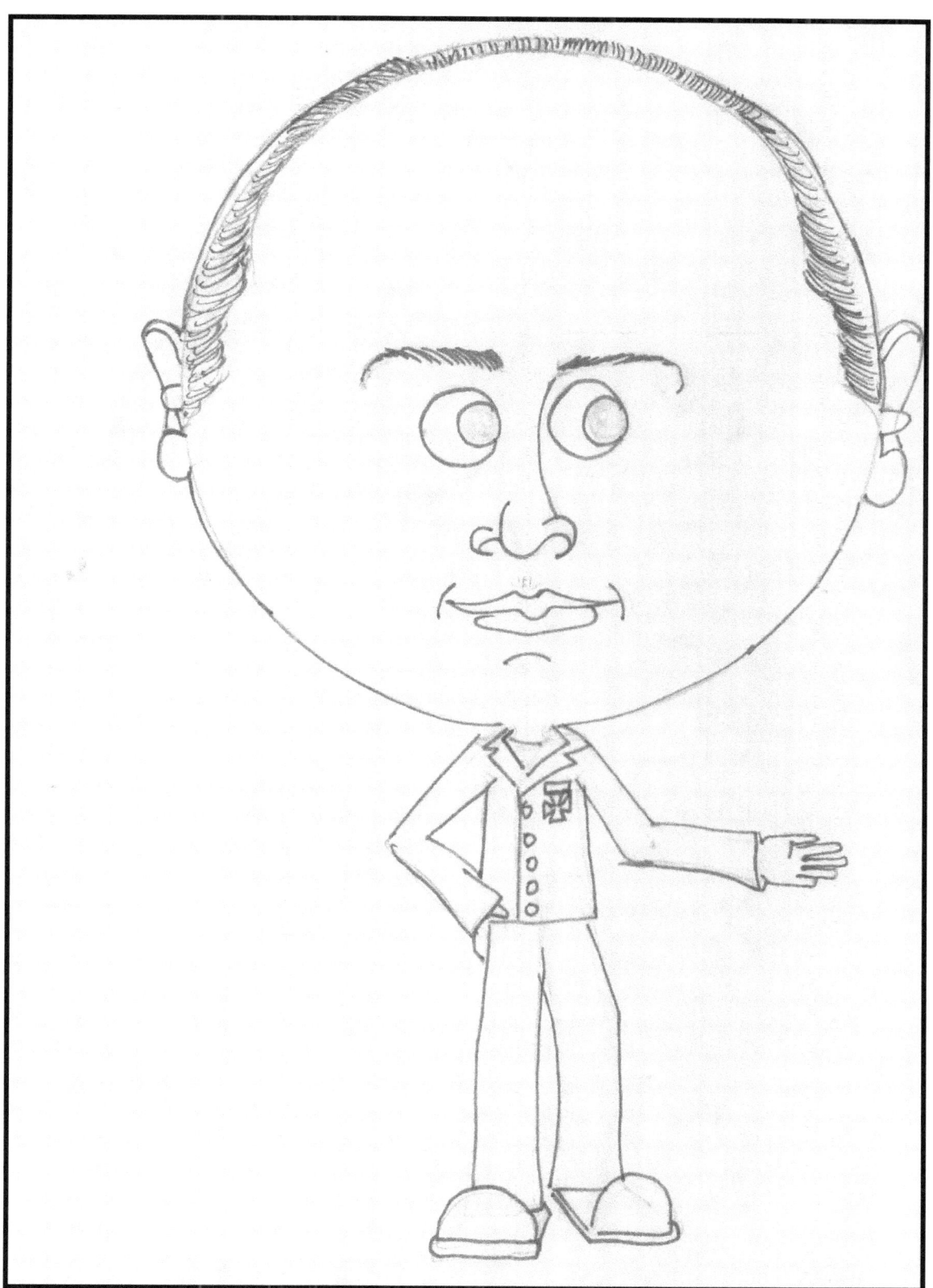

Nicholas Romanov

Mustachioed fox walks within white

   walls

Who works with jerks holding guns and

   wearing bloodied shirts

Workers and Jews know no news to

   unanswered calls

The assassin's gun ends your run.

   Now you know how it hurts.

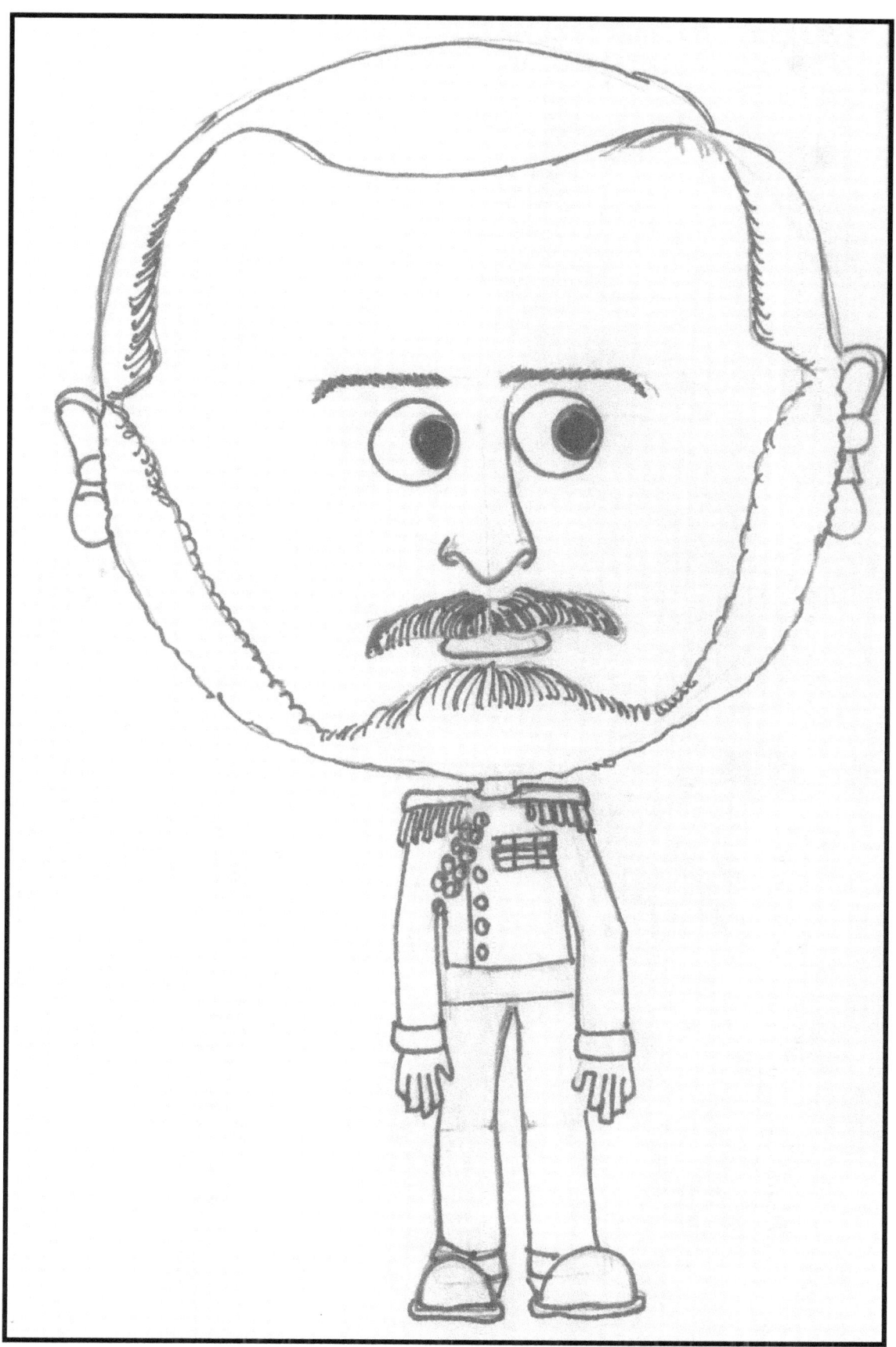

Vladimir Lenin

He was born a revolutionary

Not permitted to be stationary

He spread hope to the weakened at the
   train station

Look at the father of the Communist
   nation.

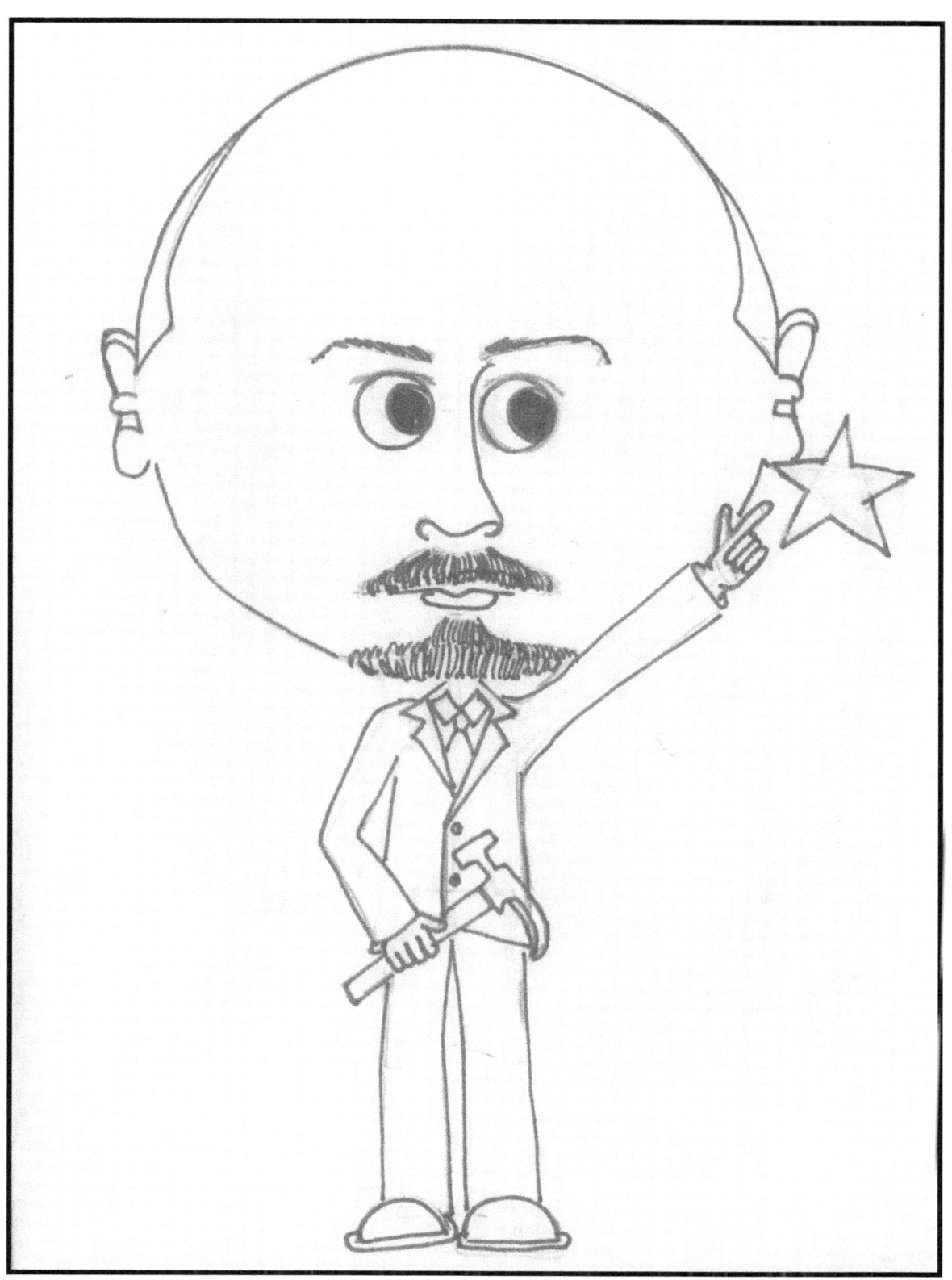

Tomas de Torquemada

Welcome to the Spanish Inquisition

and heretics posed in weird positions

This monk's monastery seems rather

    scary

And all of Europe feels unsafe and wary.

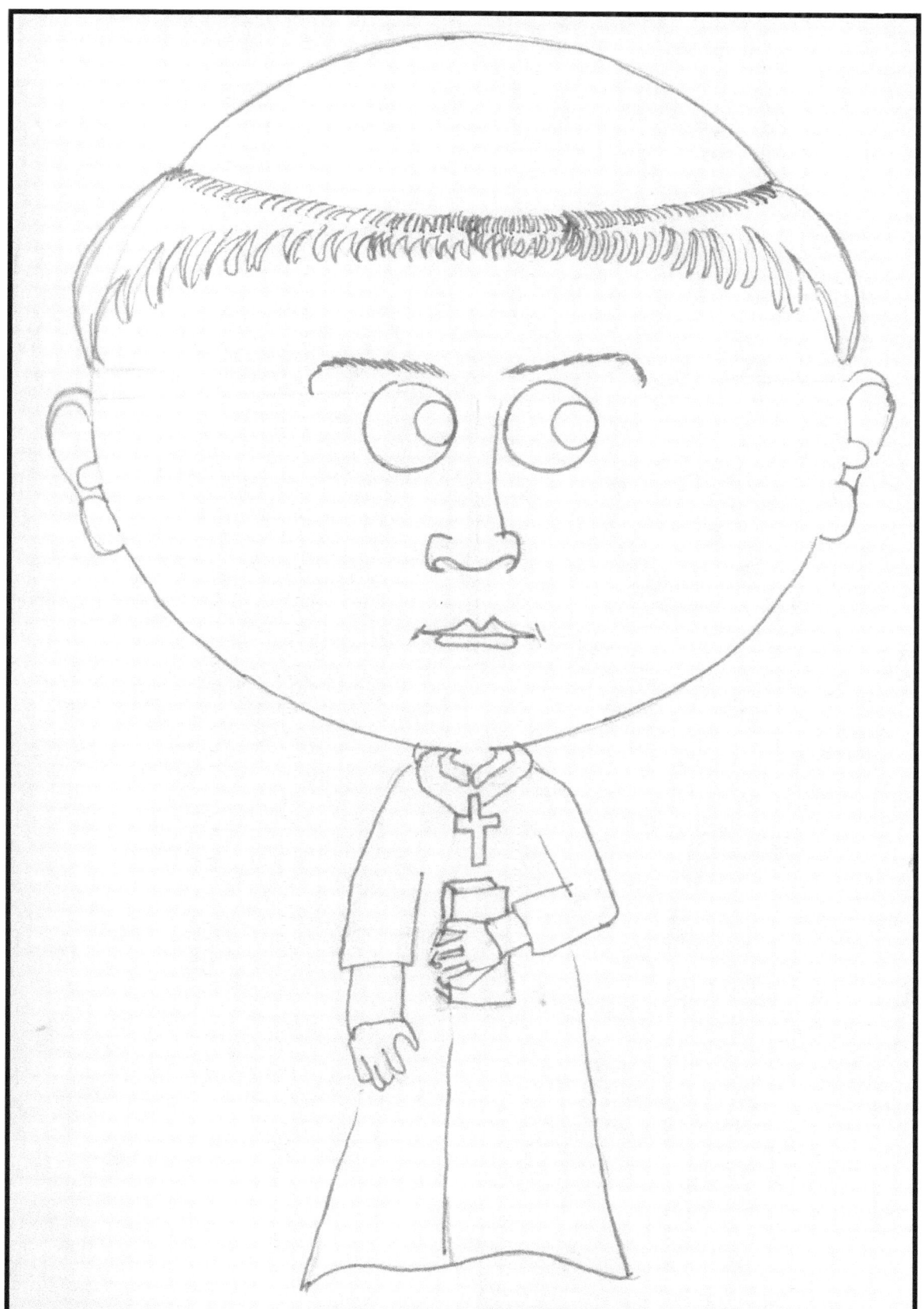

Osama bin laden

Disenchanted Djin destroyed on a whim

Made it clear, again and again

Opposition of the Jihad nation

Could end with global extermination

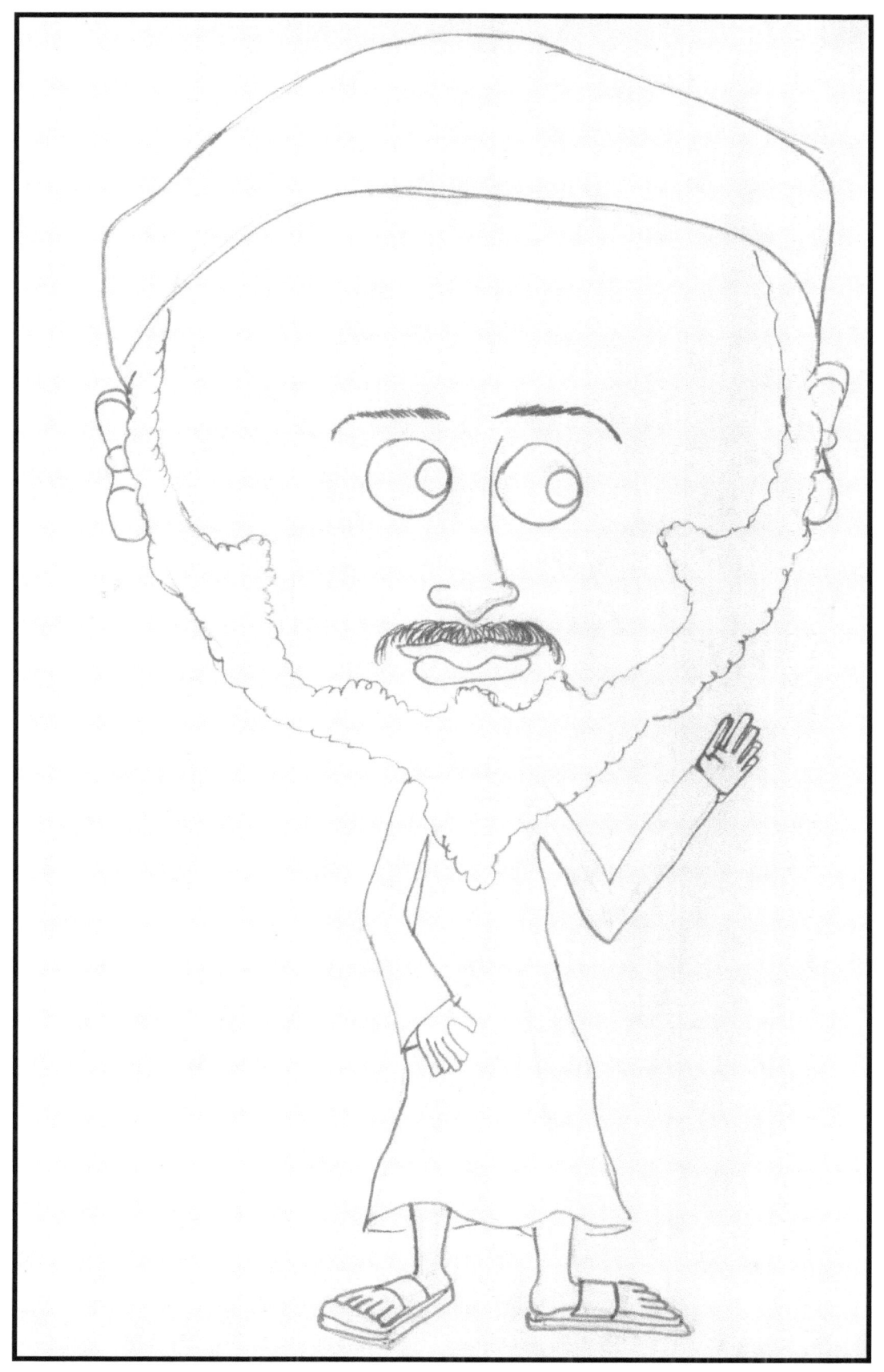

Saloth Sar

Grief's new leaf sees an idiotic edge

Eschew knowledge for a bamboo
college

Here's year zero for Pol Pot the hero

We work for rice in long hours and long
rows.

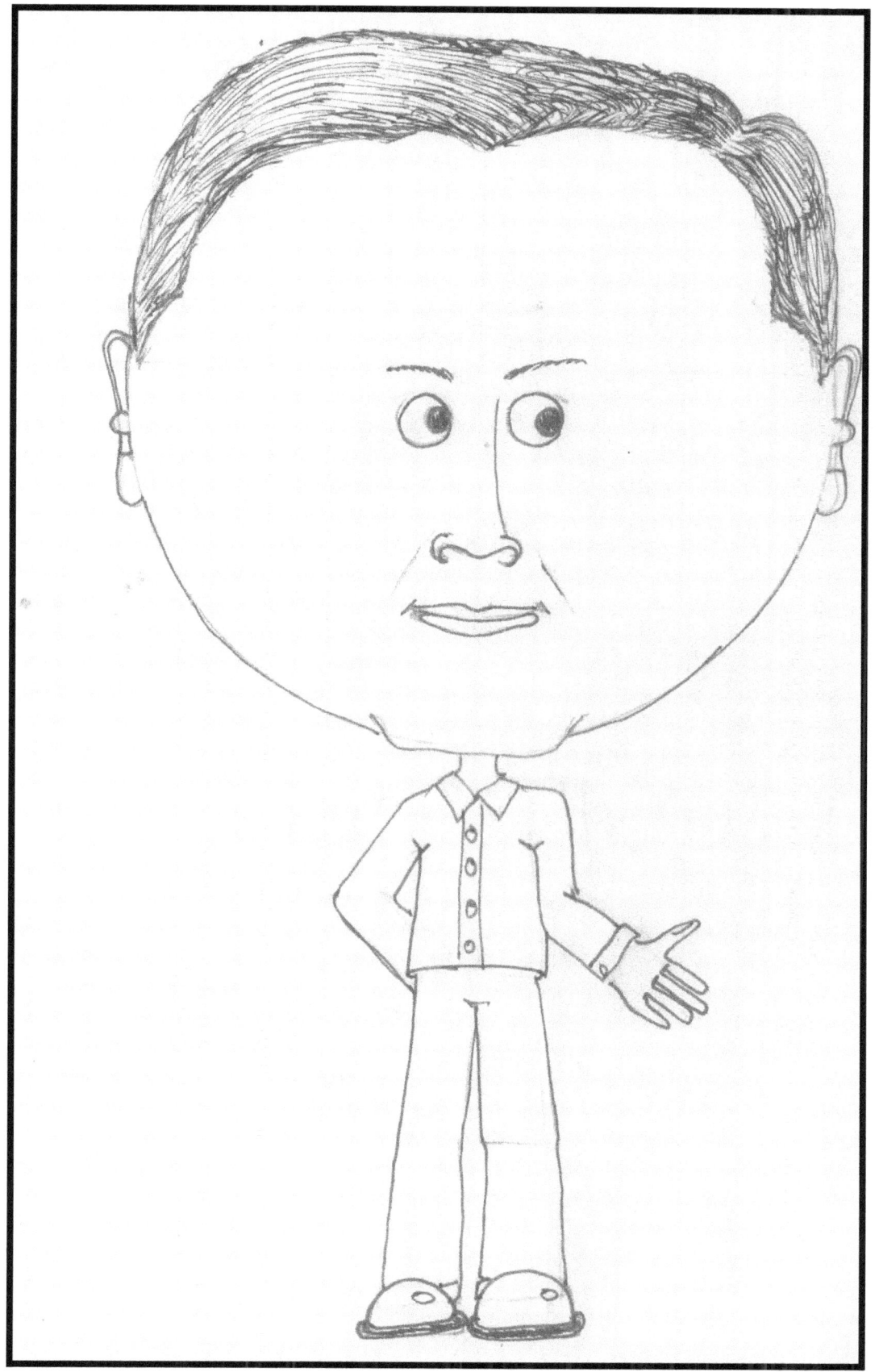

Moammar-al-Quaddafy

Try to incite all nations with aplomb

Praise foreign civil wars while you
squash yours

My Chinese brothers, can you spare a
bomb?

See Scotland's sky shower metallic
doors.

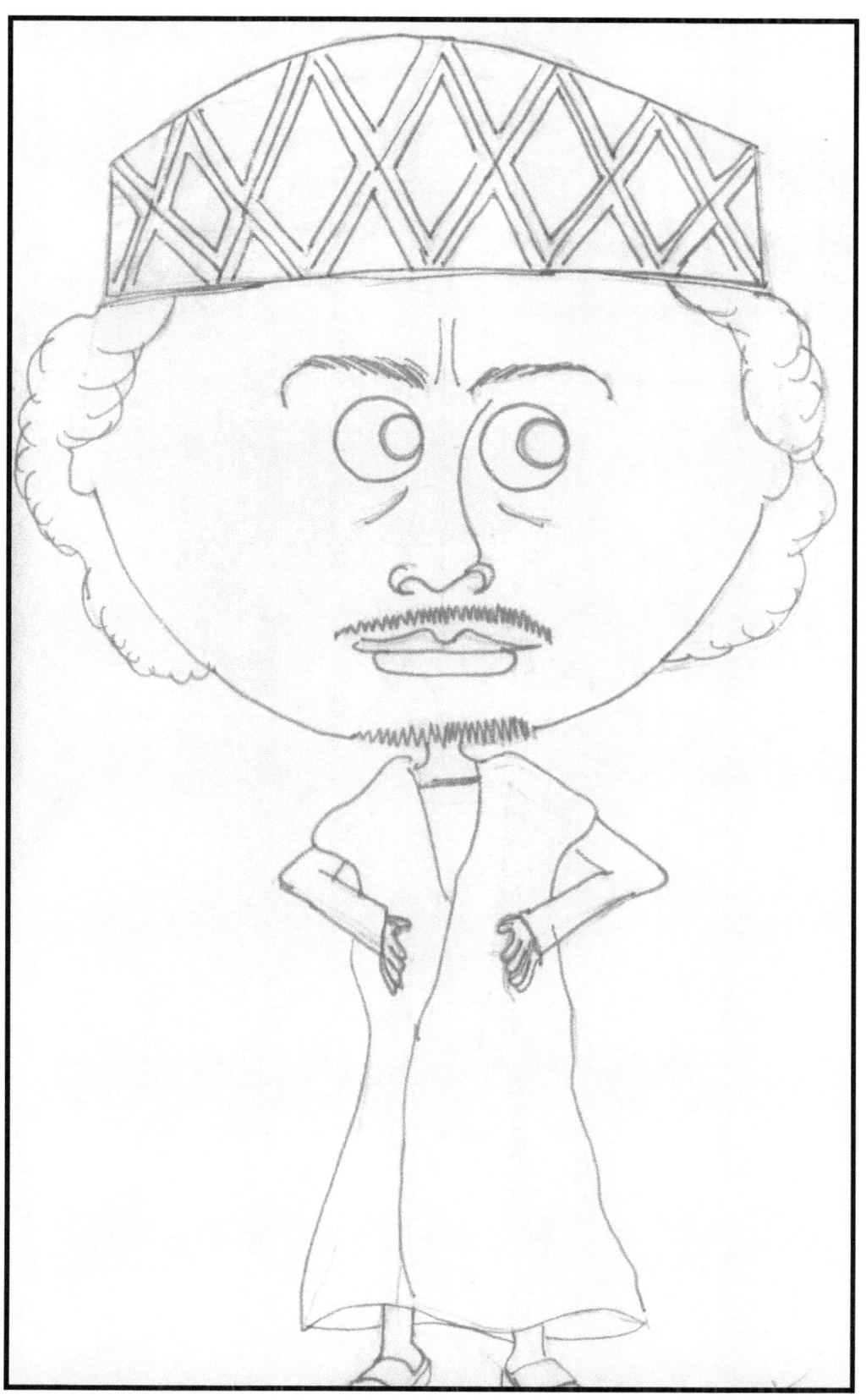

Mehmet Talat and Ismail Enver

Forsake your faith for Armenian graves

Lifeless delight in this civic mistreatment

Bathe experts enslaved in necrotic
staves

Meant for more than a martyr's
monument

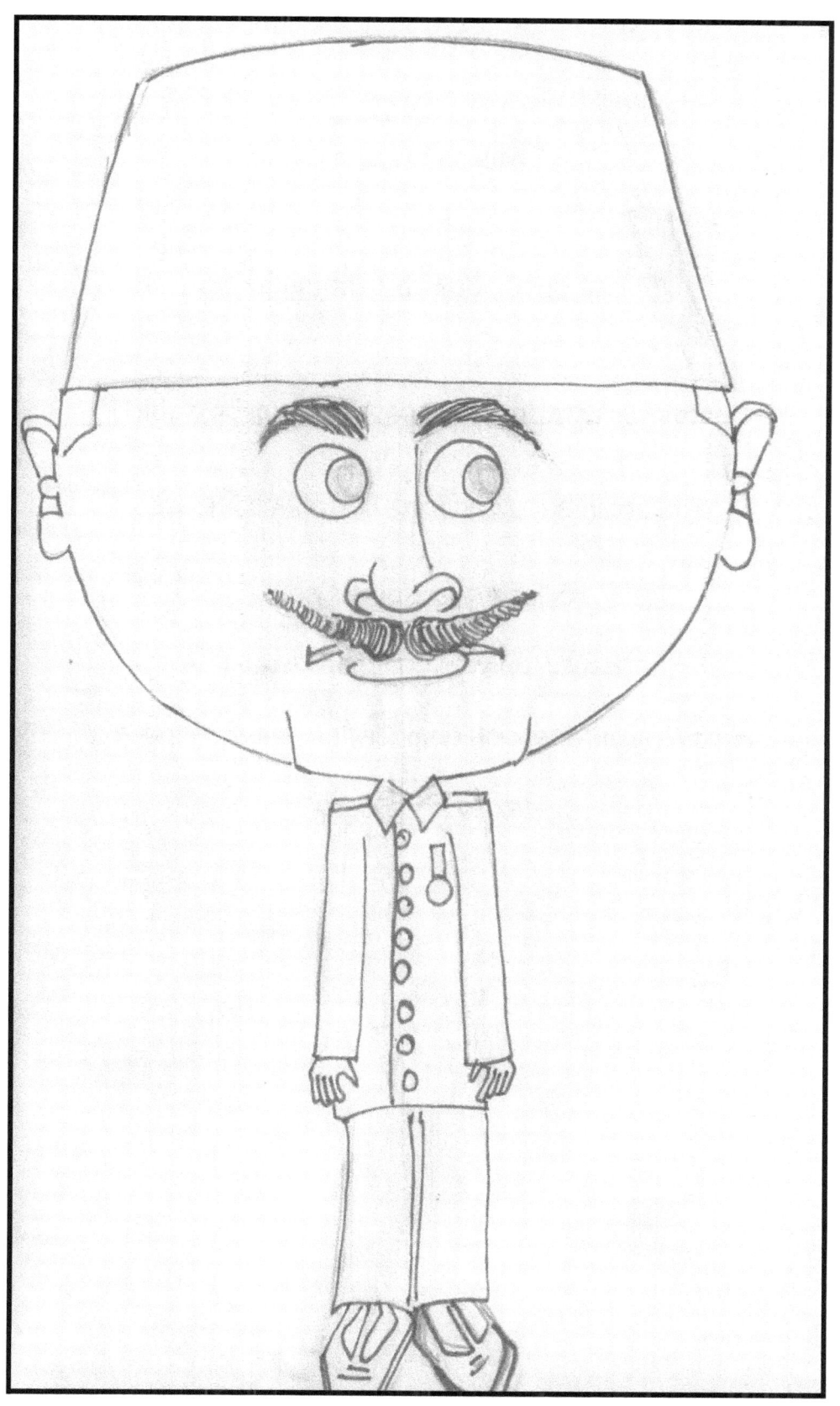

www.ingramcontent.com/pod-product-compliance
Lightning Source LLC
Chambersburg PA
CBHW080614190526
45169CB00007B/3012